Bodies of Water

S0-AQL-213

Oceans and Seas

Cassie Mayer

Heinemann Library
Chicago, Illinois

© 2008 Heinemann Library
a division of Capstone Global Library, LLC
Chicago, Illinois

Customer Service 800-747-4992
Visit our website at www.heinemannraintree.com

All rights reserved. No part of this publication may be reproduced or transmitted in any form or by any means, electronic or mechanical, including photocopying, recording, taping, or any information storage and retrieval system, without permission in writing from the publisher.

Designed by Joanna Hinton-Malivoire
Photo research by Erica Martin
Printed in the United States of America in Eau Claire, Wisconsin

042014
008150RP

ISBN-10: 1-4034-9363 (hc)
ISBN-10: 1-4034-9367-7 (pb)

The Library of Congress has cataloged the first edition of this book as follows:
Mayer, Cassie.
  Oceans and seas / Cassie Mayer.
     p. cm. -- (Bodies of water)
  Includes bibliographical references and index.
  ISBN-13: 978-1-4034-9363-7 (hc)
  ISBN-13: 978-1-4034-9367-5 (pb)
  1. Ocean--Juvenile literature. I. Title.
  GC21.5.M39 2006
  551.46--dc22

                          2006034283

Acknowledgements
The publishers would like to thank the following for permission to reproduce photographs: Alamy pp. **5** (eye35.com), **18** (Michael Diggin); Corbis pp. **4** (NASA), **10** (Blaine Harrington III), **13** (Zefa/Gary Bell), **15** (Steve Terrill), **19** (Zefa/ Wilfried Krecichwost), **20** (Onne van der Wal), **23** (barge: Onne van der Wal; kelp: Zefa/Gary Bell; beach: Zefa/Wilfried Krecichwost); Getty Images pp. **6** (Raphael Van Butsele), **14**, **21** (Alison Langley); Jupiter Images pp. **7** (Dynamic Graphics), **11**; Nature Picture Library p. **12** (Georgette Douwma); Photolibrary pp. **16** (Sue Scott), **17** (Sue Scott).

Cover photograph reproduced with permission of Corbis (Zefa/Jason Hosking). Back cover photograph reproduced with permission of Corbis (Zefa/Wilfried Krecichwost).

Every effort has been made to contact copyright holders of any material reproduced in this book. Any omissions will be rectified in subsequent printings if notice is given to the publishers.

Contents

Oceans

water

Most of the Earth is covered by water.

Most of this water is in oceans.

An ocean is a large area covered by water.

Oceans have salt water.

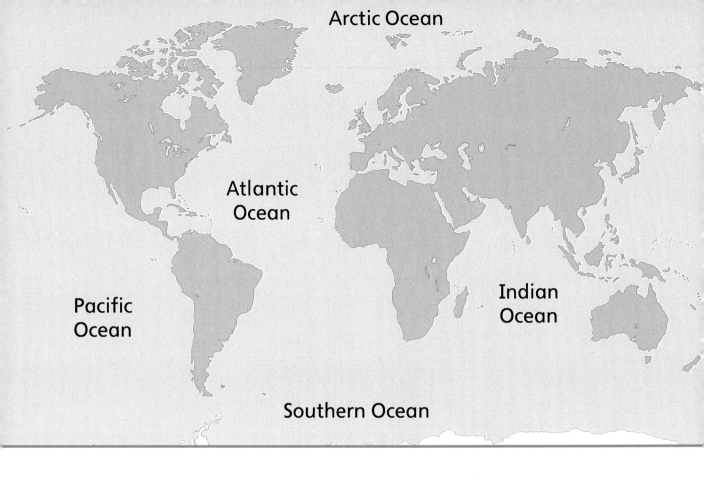

Arctic Ocean

Atlantic
Ocean

Pacific
Ocean

Indian
Ocean

Southern Ocean

There are five oceans.

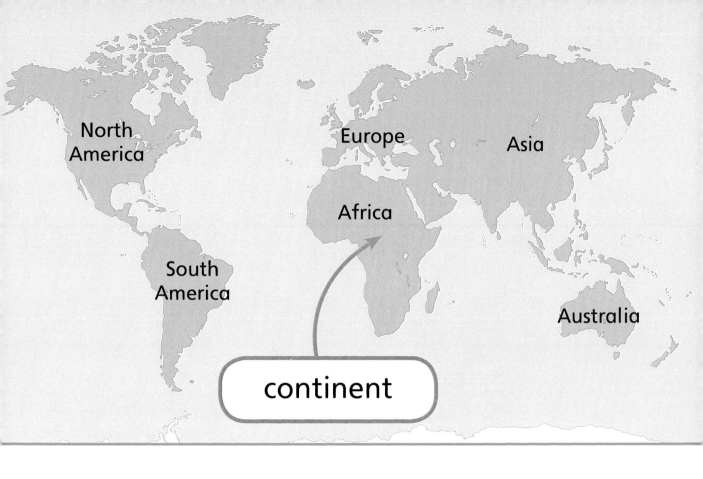

Oceans are divided by pieces of land. These pieces of land are called continents.

Seas

sea

Most seas are smaller parts of oceans.

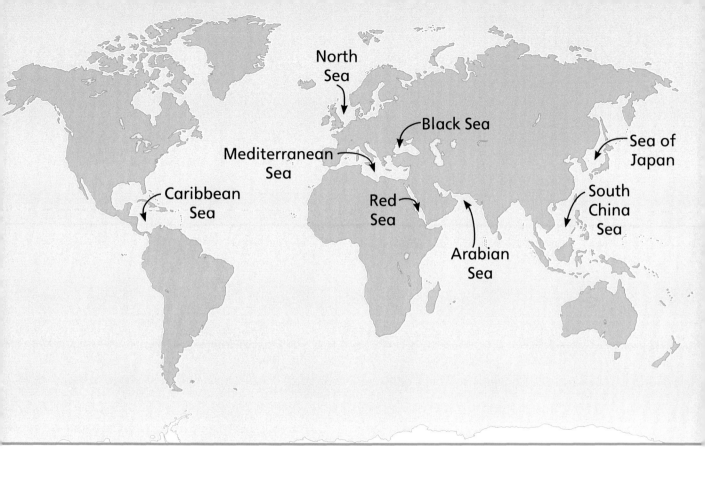

There are many seas.

Ocean Life

Oceans have many animals.

seaweed

Oceans have many plants.

Ocean Movements

Wind moves across oceans.

Wind makes waves.

Waves wear away rocks near
the ocean.

Ocean waters rise near land.

Ocean waters fall near land.
This rise and fall is called a tide.

High tides have high water levels.

Low tides have low water levels.

How We Use Oceans

People use oceans to move goods.

People use oceans to reach
new places.

Ocean Facts

The Pacific Ocean is the largest ocean in the world.

The Mariana Trench is the deepest part of the ocean. It is in the Pacific Ocean.

Picture Glossary

 **continent** a large piece of land

 **goods** things that people buy and sell

 **tide** a change in ocean water level

 **seaweed** a plant in the ocean

Index

Note to Parents and Teachers
This series introduces bodies of water and their unique characteristics. Discuss with children bodies of water they are already familiar with, pointing out different bodies of water that exist in the area in which they live. Use the maps featured on pages 8, 9, and 11 to introduce students to basic map-reading skills, such as the use of color to differentiate between land and water.

The text has been chosen with the advice of a literacy expert to enable beginning readers success in reading independently or with moderate support. An expert in the field of geography was consulted to ensure accurate content. You can support children's nonfiction literacy skills by helping them use the table of contents, headings, picture glossary, and index.